Independent Schools
Examinations Board

LATIN POCKET NOTES

R C Bass

Editor: Stephen Anderson

Independent Schools
Examinations Board

www.galorepark.co.uk

GALORE PARK

First published in 2011 by Galore Park Publishing Limited
Hodder & Stoughton Limited
Carmelite House
50 Victoria Embankment
London EC4Y 0DZ
www.galorepark.co.uk

ISBN: 978 1 907047 71 8

Impression 15 14 13 12 11 10
Year 2025 2024 2023 2022 2021

Details of other ISEB revision guides, publications and examination papers,
and Galore Park publications are available at www.galorepark.co.uk

Front cover image of a 1st century AD bronze brooch with the Tenth Legion insignia, gift
of Jack and Jane Weprin to The Israel Museum, Jerusalem (Bridgeman Art Library).

CONTENTS

INTRODUCTION

This pocket-sized guide contains all the grammar and syntax prescribed for each of the three Common Entrance levels. It can be used not only as a companion to any course book but also as a revision aid as examination time approaches.

SECTION 1: GRAMMATICAL TERMS

adjective	A word which describes nouns. e.g. **bonus** = *good*, **tristis** = *sad*.
adverb	A word which describes verbs. e.g. **celeriter** = *quickly*, **statim** = *immediately*
cardinal number	**unus** = *one*, **duo** = *two*, **tres** = *three* etc. Note carefully the difference between this and an ordinal number.
case	nominative (subject), vocative (person spoken to), accusative (object), genitive (of), dative (to or for) or ablative (by, with, from).
comparative adjective	An adjective ending in **–or** meaning *more…* e.g. **altior** = *higher*.
conjugation	A family of verbs. e.g. **amo** (1) is in the first conjugation; **audio** (4) is in the fourth conjugation.
conjunction	A joining word. e.g. **et** = *and*, **sed** = *but*.
declension	A family of nouns. e.g. **puella** = *girl* is in the first declension; **servus** = *slave* is in the second declension; **rex** = *king* is in the third declension. There are five declensions in all.

gender	Whether a noun, adjective or pronoun is masculine, feminine or neuter.
imperative	An order. e.g. **audi!** = *listen!* **amate!** = *love!*
infinitive	A 'to' word, the second principal part of a verb, usually ending in **–re** in Latin. e.g. **amare** = *to love*. But beware of **esse** = *to be*.
number	Whether a noun, verb, adjective or pronoun is singular or plural.
ordinal number	**primus** = *first,* **secundus** = *second,* **tertius** = *third* and so on. Note carefully the difference between this and a cardinal number.
past participle passive	The supine with the final **–m** replaced with an **–s**. e.g. supine **amatum** gives the past participle passive **amatus** = *having been loved*.
person	1st person singular = *I* 2nd person singular = *you* 3rd person singular = *he, she, it* 1st person plural = *we* 2nd person plural = *you* 3rd person plural = *they*

prepositions	Little words like **cum** = *with*, **ad** = *to, towards*, **in** = *in*. In Latin, some prepositions are followed by accusative nouns, others by ablative nouns.
relative pronoun	Who/which (**qui, quae, quod**).
superlative adjective	An adjective ending in **–issimus** or **–errimus**, meaning *very* or *most*. e.g. **altissimus** = *very high, highest*.
supine	The fourth principal part, ending in **–um**. e.g. **amatum**.
tense	Present, future, imperfect, perfect or pluperfect.
voice	Active or passive. e.g. **amo** = *I love* is in the active voice, but **amor** = *I am loved* is in the passive voice.

SECTION 2: NOUNS

Summary of case usage

name of case	job	examples
nominative	subject (doer) of verb	<u>servus</u> laborat. *The slave is working.*
	with the verb 'to be'.	Marcus est <u>servus</u>. *Marcus is a slave.*
vocative	person spoken to	quid facis, <u>serve</u>? *Slave, what are you doing?*
accusative	object (receiver) of verb	<u>servum</u> punio. *I am punishing the slave.*
	after prepositions like **ad, per**.	ad <u>servum</u> currit. *He is running towards the slave.*
	time (for how long)	mul<u>tas</u> ho<u>ras</u> ambulabam. *I was walking for many hours.*

name of case	job	examples
genitive	*of*	dominus <u>servi</u> est saevus. *The master of the slave is cruel.*
dative	*to, for*	pecuniam <u>servo</u> dat. *He gives money to the slave.*
ablative	*by, with, from*	puerum <u>gladio</u> vulnerat. *He wounds the boy with his sword.*
	after prepositions like **cum, in**.	cum <u>servo</u> pugnat. *He is fighting with the slave.*
	time (when)	medi<u>a</u> noct<u>e</u> discessit. *He left in the middle of the night.*

Summary of nouns

Level 1: declensions 1 and 2 • Level 2: declension 3 • Level 3: declension 5

declension	1	2	2	2	2
gender	f	m	m	m	n
	girl	*lord/master*	*boy*	*field*	*war*
SINGULAR					
nominative	puell**a**	domin**us**	pu**er**	ag**er**	bell**um**
vocative	puell**a**	domin**e**	pu**er**	ag**er**	bell**um**
accusative	puell**am**	domin**um**	puer**um**	agr**um**	bell**um**
genitive	puell**ae**	domin**i**	puer**i**	agr**i**	bell**i**
dative	puell**ae**	domin**o**	puer**o**	agr**o**	bell**o**
ablative	puell**a**	domin**o**	puer**o**	agr**o**	bell**o**
PLURAL	*girls*	*lords/masters*	*boys*	*fields*	*wars*
nominative	puell**ae**	domin**i**	puer**i**	agr**i**	bell**a**
vocative	puell**ae**	domin**i**	puer**i**	agr**i**	bell**a**
accusative	puell**as**	domin**os**	puer**os**	agr**os**	bell**a**
genitive	puell**arum**	domin**orum**	puer**orum**	agr**orum**	bell**orum**
dative	puell**is**	domin**is**	puer**is**	agr**is**	bell**is**
ablative	puell**is**	domin**is**	puer**is**	agr**is**	bell**is**

declension	3	3	5
gender	m/f	n	m/f
	king (m)	*name*	*thing* (f)
SINGULAR			
nominative	rex	nomen	res
vocative	rex	nomen	res
accusative	reg**em**	nomen	r**em**
genitive	reg**is**	nomin**is**	re**i**
dative	reg**i**	nomin**i**	re**i**
ablative	reg**e**	nomin**e**	r**e**
PLURAL	*kings*	*names*	*things*
nominative	reg**es**	nomin**a**	res
vocative	reg**es**	nomin**a**	res
accusative	reg**es**	nomin**a**	res
genitive	reg**um**	nomin**um**	re**rum**
dative	reg**ibus**	nomin**ibus**	re**bus**
ablative	reg**ibus**	nomin**ibus**	re**bus**

LEVEL
2

LEVEL
3

SECTION 3: ADJECTIVES

Adjectives in –us e.g. **bonus** = *good*

	masculine	feminine	neuter
SINGULAR			
nominative	bon**us**	bon**a**	bon**um**
vocative	bon**e**	bon**a**	bon**um**
accusative	bon**um**	bon**am**	bon**um**
genitive	bon**i**	bon**ae**	bon**i**
dative	bon**o**	bon**ae**	bon**o**
ablative	bon**o**	bon**a**	bon**o**
PLURAL			
nominative	bon**i**	bon**ae**	bon**a**
vocative	bon**i**	bon**ae**	bon**a**
accusative	bon**os**	bon**as**	bon**a**
genitive	bon**orum**	bon**arum**	bon**orum**
dative	bon**is**	bon**is**	bon**is**
ablative	bon**is**	bon**is**	bon**is**

Adjectives in –er (keeping the e) e.g. **miser** = *miserable*

	masculine	feminine	neuter
SINGULAR			
nominative	miser	misera	miserum
vocative	miser	misera	miserum
accusative	miserum	miseram	miserum
genitive	miseri	miserae	miseri
dative	misero	miserae	misero
ablative	misero	misera	misero
PLURAL			
nominative	miseri	miserae	misera
vocative	miseri	miserae	misera
accusative	miseros	miseras	misera
genitive	miserorum	miserarum	miserorum
dative	miseris	miseris	miseris
ablative	miseris	miseris	miseris

Adjectives in –er (dropping the e) e.g. **pulcher** = *beautiful*

	masculine	feminine	neuter
SINGULAR			
nominative	pulcher	pulchra	pulchrum
vocative	pulcher	pulchra	pulchrum
accusative	pulchrum	pulchram	pulchrum
genitive	pulchri	pulchrae	pulchri
dative	pulchro	pulchrae	pulchro
ablative	pulchro	pulchra	pulchro
PLURAL			
nominative	pulchri	pulchrae	pulchra
vocative	pulchri	pulchrae	pulchra
accusative	pulchros	pulchras	pulchra
genitive	pulchrorum	pulchrarum	pulchrorum
dative	pulchris	pulchris	pulchris
ablative	pulchris	pulchris	pulchris

Third declension adjectives in –is e.g. **tristis** = *sad/gloomy*

	masculine	feminine	neuter
SINGULAR			
nominative	trist**is**	trist**is**	trist**e**
vocative	trist**is**	trist**is**	trist**e**
accusative	trist**em**	trist**em**	trist**e**
genitive	trist**is**	trist**is**	trist**is**
dative	trist**i**	trist**i**	trist**i**
ablative	trist**i**	trist**i**	trist**i**
PLURAL			
nominative	trist**es**	trist**es**	trist**ia**
vocative	trist**es**	trist**es**	trist**ia**
accusative	trist**es**	trist**es**	trist**ia**
genitive	trist**ium**	trist**ium**	trist**ium**
dative	trist**ibus**	trist**ibus**	trist**ibus**
ablative	trist**ibus**	trist**ibus**	trist**ibus**

Third declension adjectives in **–x** e.g. **felix** = *fortunate*

	masculine	feminine	neuter
SINGULAR			
nominative	felix	felix	felix
vocative	felix	felix	felix
accusative	felic**em**	felic**em**	felix
genitive	felic**is**	felic**is**	felic**is**
dative	felic**i**	felic**i**	felic**i**
ablative	felic**i**	felic**i**	felic**i**
PLURAL			
nominative	felic**es**	felic**es**	felic**ia**
vocative	felic**es**	felic**es**	felic**ia**
accusative	felic**es**	felic**es**	felic**ia**
genitive	felic**ium**	felic**ium**	felic**ium**
dative	felic**ibus**	felic**ibus**	felic**ibus**
ablative	felic**ibus**	felic**ibus**	felic**ibus**

Third declension adjectives in –ns e.g. **ingens** = *huge*

	masculine	feminine	neuter
SINGULAR			
nominative	ingens	ingens	ingens
vocative	ingens	ingens	ingens
accusative	ingent**em**	ingent**em**	ingens
genitive	ingent**is**	ingent**is**	ingent**is**
dative	ingent**i**	ingent**i**	ingent**i**
ablative	ingent**i**	ingent**i**	ingent**i**
PLURAL			
nominative	ingent**es**	ingent**es**	ingent**ia**
vocative	ingent**es**	ingent**es**	ingent**ia**
accusative	ingent**es**	ingent**es**	ingent**ia**
genitive	ingent**ium**	ingent**ium**	ingent**ium**
dative	ingent**ibus**	ingent**ibus**	ingent**ibus**
ablative	ingent**ibus**	ingent**ibus**	ingent**ibus**

Comparison in Latin

Here are some examples:

	positive	comparative	superlative
–us	altus = high	stem + **ior** altior = higher	stem + **issimus** altissimus = highest/very high
–er	miser = miserable pulcher = beautiful	stem + **ior** miserior = more miserable pulchrior = more beautiful	positive + **rimus** miserrimus = very miserable pulcherrimus = very beautiful
–is	fortis = brave	stem + **ior** fortior = more brave	stem + **issimus** fortissimus = very brave, the bravest
–x	felix = fortunate	stem + **ior** felicior = more fortunate	stem + **issimus** felicissimus = very fortunate
–ns	ingens = huge	stem + **ior** ingentior = more huge	stem + **issimus** ingentissimus = very huge

Comparative adjectives in –ior e.g. **altior** = *higher*

	masculine	feminine	neuter
SINGULAR			
nominative	alt**ior**	alt**ior**	alt**ius**
vocative	alt**ior**	alt**ior**	alt**ius**
accusative	alt**iorem**	alt**iorem**	alt**ius**
genitive	alt**ioris**	alt**ioris**	alt**ioris**
dative	alt**iori**	alt**iori**	alt**iori**
ablative	alt**iore**	alt**iore**	alt**iore**
PLURAL			
nominative	alt**iores**	alt**iores**	alt**iora**
vocative	alt**iores**	alt**iores**	alt**iora**
accusative	alt**iores**	alt**iores**	alt**iora**
genitive	alt**iorum**	alt**iorum**	alt**iorum**
dative	alt**ioribus**	alt**ioribus**	alt**ioribus**
ablative	alt**ioribus**	alt**ioribus**	alt**ioribus**

Irregular comparison of adjectives

positive	comparative	superlative
bonus = *good*	melior = *better*	optimus = *very good, best*
malus = *bad*	peior = *worse*	pessimus = *very bad, worst*
magnus = *big*	maior = *bigger*	maximus = *very big, biggest*
parvus = *small*	minor = *smaller*	minimus = *very small, smallest*
multus = *much, many*	plus = *more*	plurimus = *most, very many*

SECTION 4: PRONOUNS

First person pronouns: ego

(only nom. and acc. required for Level 1)

	singular		plural	
nominative	ego	*I*	nos	*we*
accusative	me	*me*	nos	*us*
genitive	mei	*of me/my*	nostrum	*of us/our*
dative	mihi	*to/for me*	nobis	*to/for us*
ablative	me	*by/with/from me*	nobis	*by/with/from us*

nb mecum   – with us (s.)
    nobisum – with us (pl.)

Second person pronouns: tu

(only nom. and acc. required for Level 1)

		singular		plural	
LEVEL 1 nominative	tu	*you*	vos	*you*
accusative	te	*you*	vos	*you*
LEVEL 2 genitive	tui	*of you/your*	vestrum	*of you/your*
dative	tibi	*to/for you*	vobis	*to/for you*
ablative	te	*by/with/from you*	vobis	*by/with/from you*

nb   tecum   = with you (s.)
     vobiscum = with you (pl.)

Third person reflexive pronoun: se

	singular		plural	
nominative	–		–	
accusative	se	*himself/herself*	se	*themselves*
genitive	sui	*of himself/herself*	sui	*of themselves*
dative	sibi	*to/for himself/herself*	sibi	*to/for themselves*
ablative	se	*by/with/from himself/herself*	se	*by/with/from themselves*

nb secum = with him/her (s.)
   secum = with them (pl.)

Third person pronoun: is, ea, id = *he, she, it*

	masculine		feminine		neuter	
SINGULAR						
nominative	is	*he*	ea	*she*	id	*it*
accusative	eum	*him*	eam	*her*	id	*it*
genitive	eius	*his*	eius	*her*	eius	*of it*
dative	ei	*to/for him*	ei	*to/for her*	ei	*to/for it*
ablative	eo	*by him*	ea	*by her*	eo	*by it*
PLURAL						
nominative	ei	*they*	eae	*they*	ea	*they*
accusative	eos	*them*	eas	*them*	ea	*them*
genitive	eorum	*their*	earum	*their*	eorum	*their*
dative	eis	*to/for them*	eis	*to/for them*	eis	*to/for them*
ablative	eis	*by them*	eis	*by them*	eis	*by them*

LEVEL
2

Demonstrative pronoun/adjective: hic, haec, hoc = *this*, plural *these*

'Demonstrative' just means 'pointing something out'. The word 'this' points to something near the speaker.

	masculine	feminine	neuter
SINGULAR			
nominative	hic	haec	hoc
accusative	hunc	hanc	hoc
genitive	huius	huius	huius
dative	huic	huic	huic
ablative	hoc	hac	hoc
PLURAL			
nominative	hi	hae	haec
accusative	hos	has	haec
genitive	horum	harum	horum
dative	his	his	his
ablative	his	his	his

LEVEL 2

Demonstrative pronoun/adjective: ille, illa, illud = *that*, plural *those*

'Demonstrative' just means 'pointing something out'. The word 'that' points to something at a distance from the speaker.

LEVEL 2

	masculine	feminine	neuter
SINGULAR			
nominative	ille	illa	illud
accusative	illum	illam	illud
genitive	illius	illius	illius
dative	illi	illi	illi
ablative	illo	illa	illo
PLURAL			
nominative	illi	illae	illa
accusative	illos	illas	illa
genitive	illorum	illarum	illorum
dative	illis	illis	illis
ablative	illis	illis	illis

The relative pronoun: qui, quae, quod = *who, which*, etc.

	masculine	feminine	neuter	
SINGULAR				
nominative	qui	quae	quod	*who, which*
accusative	quem	quam	quod	*whom, which*
genitive	cuius	cuius	cuius	*whose*
dative	cui	cui	cui	*to/for whom, to/for which*
ablative	quo	qua	quo	*by/with/from whom/which*
PLURAL				
nominative	qui	quae	quae	*who, which*
accusative	quos	quas	quae	*whom, which*
genitive	quorum	quarum	quorum	*whose*
dative	quibus	quibus	quibus	*to/for whom*
ablative	quibus	quibus	quibus	*by/with/from whom/which*

Definitive pronoun/adjective: idem, eadem, idem = *the same*

	masculine	feminine	neuter
SINGULAR			
nominative	idem	eadem	idem
accusative	eundem	eandem	idem
genitive	eiusdem	eiusdem	eiusdem
dative	eidem	eidem	eidem
ablative	eodem	eadem	eodem
PLURAL			
nominative	eidem	eaedem	eadem
accusative	eosdem	easdem	eadem
genitive	eorundem	earundem	eorundem
dative	eisdem	eisdem	eisdem
ablative	eisdem	eisdem	eisdem

Intensive pronoun/adjective: ipse, ipsa, ipsum = –self

	masculine	feminine	neuter
SINGULAR			
nominative	ipse	ipsa	ipsum
accusative	ipsum	ipsam	ipsum
genitive	ipsius	ipsius	ipsius
dative	ipsi	ipsi	ipsi
ablative	ipso	ipsa	ipso
PLURAL			
nominative	ipsi	ipsae	ipsa
accusative	ipsos	ipsas	ipsa
genitive	ipsorum	ipsarum	ipsorum
dative	ipsis	ipsis	ipsis
ablative	ipsis	ipsis	ipsis

LEVEL 3

Examples

ego <u>ipse</u> reginam vidi.	*I saw the queen <u>myself</u>.*
regina <u>ipsa</u> venit.	*The queen <u>herself</u> came.*

SECTION 5: PREPOSITIONS

ad + accusative	*to, towards*	ad reginam ambulat. *He is walking towards the queen.*
contra + accusative	*against*	contra Romanos festinat. *He hurries against the Romans.*
per + accusative	*through, along*	per viam currit. *He is running along the road.*
prope + accusative	*near*	prope murum stat. *He is standing near the wall.*
trans + accusative	*across*	trans viam festinat. *He hurries across the road.*
a/ab + ablative	*(away) from*	ab insula navigat. *He sails away from the island.*
cum + ablative	*with*	cum amico ludit. *He is playing with a friend.*
de + ablative	*down from, about*	de periculo monet. *He warns about the danger.*
e/ex + ablative	*out of*	ex oppido currit. *He runs out of the town.*

The preposition in

This frequently causes problems, because it can be followed by an ablative word (when it means *in* or *on*) as well as by an accusative word (when it means *into*).

Examples	
in + ablative = *in, on*	equus in ag<u>ro</u> currit.
	The horse is running <u>in</u> the field.
in + accusative = *into*	equus in ag<u>rum</u> currit.
	The horse is running <u>into</u> the field.

ante + accusative	*before*	ante tempestatem timet. *He is afraid before the storm.*
circum + accusative	*around*	circum insulam navigat. *He sails around the island.*
inter + accusative	*among, between*	inter equos currit. *He runs between the horses.*
post + accusative	*after, behind*	post patrem ambulat. *He is walking behind his father.*
propter + accusative	*because of*	propter pericula fugit. *He flees because of the dangers.*
super + accusative	*above*	super aquam stat. *He is standing above the water.*
pro + ablative	*on behalf of, for, in front of*	pro domino pugnat. *He fights for his master.*
sine + ablative	*without*	sine gladio pugnat. *He is fighting without a sword.*
sub + ablative	*under*	sub equo dormit. *He is sleeping under the horse.*

SECTION 6: VERBS

Present tense

	1 *love*	**2** *warn*	**3** *rule*	**4** *hear*	**M** *take*	**sum** *be*
I	am**o**	mone**o**	reg**o**	audi**o**	capi**o**	sum
you (sing.)	ama**s**	mone**s**	reg**is**	audi**s**	capi**s**	es
he/she/it	ama**t**	mone**t**	reg**it**	audi**t**	capi**t**	est
we	ama**mus**	mone**mus**	regi**mus**	audi**mus**	capi**mus**	sumus
you (pl.)	ama**tis**	mone**tis**	regi**tis**	audi**tis**	capi**tis**	estis
they	ama**nt**	mone**nt**	reg**unt**	audi**unt**	capi**unt**	sunt

Imperfect tense

	1 *loving*	**2** *warning*	**3** *ruling*	**4** *hearing*	**M** *taking*	**sum** *was/were*
I was	ama**bam**	mone**bam**	rege**bam**	audie**bam**	capie**bam**	eram *I was*
you were	ama**bas**	mone**bas**	rege**bas**	audie**bas**	capie**bas**	eras *You were*
he/she/it was	ama**bat**	mone**bat**	rege**bat**	audie**bat**	capie**bat**	erat *He was*
we were	ama**bamus**	mone**bamus**	rege**bamus**	audie**bamus**	capie**bamus**	eramus *We were*
you were	ama**batis**	mone**batis**	rege**batis**	audie**batis**	capie**batis**	eratis *You were*
they were	ama**bant**	mone**bant**	rege**bant**	audie**bant**	capie**bant**	erant *They were*

Perfect tense

	1 *loved*	**2** *warned*	**3** *ruled*	**4** *heard*	**M** *took*	**sum** *was/were*
I	ama**vi**	monu**i**	rex**i**	audi**vi**	cep**i**	fu**i**
you (sing.)	ama**visti**	monu**isti**	rex**isti**	audi**visti**	cep**isti**	fu**isti**
he/she/it	ama**vit**	monu**it**	rex**it**	audi**vit**	cep**it**	fu**it**
we	ama**vimus**	monu**imus**	rex**imus**	audi**vimus**	cep**imus**	fu**imus**
you (pl.)	ama**vistis**	monu**istis**	rex**istis**	audi**vistis**	cep**istis**	fu**istis**
they	ama**verunt**	monu**erunt**	rex**erunt**	audi**verunt**	cep**erunt**	fu**erunt**

Present infinitives

	present		infinitive	
1	amo	*I love*	am**are**	*to love*
2	moneo	*I warn*	mon**ere**	*to warn*
3	rego	*I rule*	reg**ere**	*to rule*
4	audio	*I hear*	aud**ire**	*to hear*
M	capio	*I take*	cap**ere**	*to take*
irregular verb	sum	*I am*	esse	*to be*

31

Imperatives

	singular	plural	
1	ama	amate	*Love!*
2	mone	monete	*Warn!*
3	rege	regite	*Rule!*
4	audi	audite	*Hear!/Listen!*
M	cape	capite	*Take!*
sum	es/esto	este	*Be!*

32

Future tense

	1 *love*	**2** *warn*	**3** *rule*	**4** *hear*	**M** *take*	**sum** *be*
I will	ama**bo**	mone**bo**	reg**am**	audi**am**	capi**am**	ero
you (sing.) will	ama**bis**	mone**bis**	reg**es**	audi**es**	capi**es**	eris
he/she/it will	ama**bit**	mone**bit**	reg**et**	audi**et**	capi**et**	erit
we will	ama**bimus**	mone**bimus**	reg**emus**	audi**emus**	capi**emus**	erimus
you (pl.) will	ama**bitis**	mone**bitis**	reg**etis**	audi**etis**	capi**etis**	eritis
they will	ama**bunt**	mone**bunt**	reg**ent**	audi**ent**	capi**ent**	erunt

LEVEL 2

Pluperfect tense

	1 *loved*	**2** *warned*	**3** *ruled*	**4** *heard*	**M** *taken*	**sum** *been*
I had	amav**eram**	monu**eram**	rex**eram**	audiv**eram**	cep**eram**	fu**eram**
you (sing.) had	amav**eras**	monu**eras**	rex**eras**	audiv**eras**	cep**eras**	fu**eras**
he/she/it had	amav**erat**	monu**erat**	rex**erat**	audiv**erat**	cep**erat**	fu**erat**
we had	amav**eramus**	monu**eramus**	rex**eramus**	audiv**eramus**	cep**eramus**	fu**eramus**
you (pl.) had	amav**eratis**	monu**eratis**	rex**eratis**	audiv**eratis**	cep**eratis**	fu**eratis**
they had	amav**erant**	monu**erant**	rex**erant**	audiv**erant**	cep**erant**	fu**erant**

Irregular verb: possum = *I am able/I can*

	present *can*	**imperfect** *could*	**perfect** *could*	**future** *will be able*	**pluperfect** *had been able*
I	possum	poteram	potui	potero	potueram
you (sing.)	potes	poteras	potuisti	poteris	potueras
he/she/it	potest	poterat	potuit	poterit	potuerat
we	possumus	poteramus	potuimus	poterimus	potueramus
you (pl.)	potestis	poteratis	potuistis	poteritis	potueratis
they	possunt	poterant	potuerunt	poterunt	potuerant
infinitive (*to*)	posse				

Irregular verb: eo = *I go*

	present *go*	imperfect *was/were going*	perfect *went*	future *will go*	pluperfect *had gone*
I	eo	ibam	ii/ivi	ibo	ieram/iveram
you (sing.)	is	ibas	iisti/ivisti	ibis	ieras/iveras
he/she/it	it	ibat	iit/ivit	ibit	ierat/iverat
we	imus	ibamus	iimus/ivimus	ibimus	ieramus/iveramus
you (pl.)	itis	ibatis	iistis/ivistis	ibitis	ieratis/iveratis
they	eunt	ibant	ierunt/iverunt	ibunt	ierant/iverant
infinitive (*to*)	ire				
imperatives:					
singular	i				
plural	ite				

Summary of regular passives

	1 *loved*	**2** *warned*	**3** *ruled*	**4** *heard*	**M** *taken*
present					
I am	am**or**	mone**or**	reg**or**	aud**ior**	cap**ior**
you (sing.) are	ama**ris**	mone**ris**	reg**eris**	aud**iris**	cap**eris**
he/she/it is	ama**tur**	mone**tur**	reg**itur**	aud**itur**	cap**itur**
we are	ama**mur**	mone**mur**	reg**imur**	aud**imur**	cap**imur**
you (pl.) are	ama**mini**	mone**mini**	reg**imini**	aud**imini**	cap**imini**
they are	ama**ntur**	mone**ntur**	reg**untur**	aud**iuntur**	cap**iuntur**
imperfect					
I was being	ama**bar**	mone**bar**	rege**bar**	audie**bar**	capie**bar**
you (sing.) were being	ama**baris**	mone**baris**	rege**baris**	audie**baris**	capie**baris**
he/she/it was being	ama**batur**	mone**batur**	rege**batur**	audie**batur**	capie**batur**
we were being	ama**bamur**	mone**bamur**	rege**bamur**	audie**bamur**	capie**bamur**
you (pl.) were being	ama**bamini**	mone**bamini**	rege**bamini**	audie**bamini**	capie**bamini**
they were being	ama**bantur**	mone**bantur**	rege**bantur**	audie**bantur**	capie**bantur**

perfect	loved	warned	ruled	heard	taken
I was	ama**tus** sum	moni**tus** sum	rec**tus** sum	audi**tus** sum	cap**tus** sum
you (sing.) were	ama**tus** es	moni**tus** es	rec**tus** es	audi**tus** es	cap**tus** es
he/she/it was	ama**tus** est	moni**tus** est	rec**tus** est	audi**tus** est	cap**tus** est
we were	ama**ti** sumus	moni**ti** sumus	rec**ti** sumus	audi**ti** sumus	cap**ti** sumus
you (pl.) were	ama**ti** estis	moni**ti** estis	rec**ti** estis	audi**ti** estis	cap**ti** estis
they were	ama**ti** sunt	moni**ti** sunt	rec**ti** sunt	audi**ti** sunt	cap**ti** sunt
future					
I will be	ama**bor**	mone**bor**	reg**ar**	audi**ar**	capi**ar**
you (sing.) will be	ama**beris**	mone**beris**	reg**eris**	audi**eris**	capi**eris**
he/she/it will be	ama**bitur**	mone**bitur**	reg**etur**	audi**etur**	capi**etur**
we will be	ama**bimur**	mone**bimur**	reg**emur**	audi**emur**	capi**emur**
you (pl.) will be	ama**bimini**	mone**bimini**	reg**emini**	audi**emini**	capi**emini**
they will be	ama**buntur**	mone**buntur**	reg**entur**	audi**entur**	capi**entur**
pluperfect					
I had been	ama**tus** eram	moni**tus** eram	rec**tus** eram	audi**tus** eram	cap**tus** eram
you (sing.) had been	ama**tus** eras	moni**tus** eras	rec**tus** eras	audi**tus** eras	cap**tus** eras
he/she/it had been	ama**tus** erat	moni**tus** erat	rec**tus** erat	audi**tus** erat	cap**tus** erat
we had been	ama**ti** eramus	moni**ti** eramus	rec**ti** eramus	audi**ti** eramus	cap**ti** eramus
you (pl.) had been	ama**ti** eratis	moni**ti** eratis	rec**ti** eratis	audi**ti** eratis	cap**ti** eratis
they had been	ama**ti** erant	moni**ti** erant	rec**ti** erant	audi**ti** erant	cap**ti** erant

Imperfect subjunctive active

1 amo, amare	2 moneo, monere	3 rego, regere	4 audio, audire	M capio, capere	to be sum, esse
amare**m**	monere**m**	regere**m**	audire**m**	capere**m**	esse**m**
amare**s**	monere**s**	regere**s**	audire**s**	capere**s**	esse**s**
amare**t**	monere**t**	regere**t**	audire**t**	capere**t**	esse**t**
amare**mus**	monere**mus**	regere**mus**	audire**mus**	capere**mus**	esse**mus**
amare**tis**	monere**tis**	regere**tis**	audire**tis**	capere**tis**	esse**tis**
amare**nt**	monere**nt**	regere**nt**	audire**nt**	capere**nt**	esse**nt**

Imperfect subjunctive passive

1 amo, amare	2 moneo, monere	3 rego, regere	4 audio, audire	M capio, capere
amare**r**	monere**r**	regere**r**	audire**r**	capere**r**
amare**ris**	monere**ris**	regere**ris**	audire**ris**	capere**ris**
amare**tur**	monere**tur**	regere**tur**	audire**tur**	capere**tur**
amare**mur**	monere**mur**	regere**mur**	audire**mur**	capere**mur**
amare**mini**	monere**mini**	regere**mini**	audire**mini**	capere**mini**
amare**ntur**	monere**ntur**	regere**ntur**	audire**ntur**	capere**ntur**

Present participles

1	amans, amantis	*loving*
2	monens, monentis	*warning, advising*
3	regens, regentis	*ruling*
4	audiens, audientis	*listening, hearing*
M	capiens, capientis	*taking*

	masculine	feminine	neuter
SINGULAR			
nominative	amans	amans	amans
vocative	amans	amans	amans
accusative	amant**em**	amant**em**	amans
genitive	amant**is**	amant**is**	amant**is**
dative	amant**i**	amant**i**	amant**i**
ablative	amant**i**	amant**i**	amant**i**
PLURAL			
nominative	amant**es**	amant**es**	amant**ia**
vocative	amant**es**	amant**es**	amant**ia**
accusative	amant**es**	amant**es**	amant**ia**
genitive	amant**ium**	amant**ium**	amant**ium**
dative	amant**ibus**	amant**ibus**	amant**ibus**
ablative	amant**ibus**	amant**ibus**	amant**ibus**

LEVEL
3

Past participles

1	amatus, –a, –um	*having been loved*
2	monitus, –a, –um	*having been warned*
3	rectus, –a, –um	*having been ruled*
4	auditus, –a, –um	*having been heard*
M	captus, –a, –um	*having been taken*

Irregular verb: fero, ferre, tuli, latum = I bear, I carry

ACTIVE	present *carry*	imperfect *was/were carrying*	perfect *carried*	future *will carry*	pluperfect *had carried*
I	fero	ferebam	tuli	feram	tuleram
you (sing.)	fers	ferebas	tulisti	feres	tuleras
he/she/it	fert	ferebat	tulit	feret	tulerat
we	ferimus	ferebamus	tulimus	feremus	tuleramus
you (pl.)	fertis	ferebatis	tulistis	feretis	tuleratis
they	ferunt	ferebant	tulerunt	ferent	tulerant
infinitive (*to*)	ferre				
imperatives:					
singular	fer				
plural	ferte				

PASSIVE	present *am/is/are carried*	imperfect *was/were being carried*	perfect *was/were carried*	future *will be carried*	pluperfect *had been carried*
I	feror	ferebar	latus sum	ferar	latus eram
you (sing.)	ferris	ferebaris	latus es	fereris	latus eras
he/she/it	fertur	ferebatur	latus est	feretur	latus erat
we	ferimur	ferebamur	lati sumus	feremur	lati eramus
you (pl.)	ferimini	ferebamini	lati estis	feremini	lati eratis
they	feruntur	ferebantur	lati sunt	ferentur	lati erant

LEVEL
3

Irregular verb: volo, velle, volui = *I wish, I want*

	present *want*	imperfect *wanted*	perfect *wanted*	future *will want*	pluperfect *had wanted*
I	volo	volebam	volui	volam	volueram
you (sing.)	vis	volebas	voluisti	voles	volueras
he/she/it	vult	volebat	voluit	volet	voluerat
we	volumus	volebamus	voluimus	volemus	volueramus
you (pl.)	vultis	volebatis	voluistis	voletis	volueratis
they	volunt	volebant	voluerunt	volent	voluerant
infinitive (to)	velle				

Irregular verb: nolo, nolle, nolui = *I do not wish, I refuse*

	present *do not want*	**imperfect** *did not want*	**perfect** *did not want*	**future** *will not want*	**pluperfect** *had not wanted*
I	nolo	nolebam	nolui	nolam	nolueram
you (sing.)	non vis	nolebas	noluisti	noles	nolueras
he/she/it	non vult	nolebat	noluit	nolet	noluerat
we	nolumus	nolebamus	noluimus	nolemus	nolueramus
you (pl.)	non vultis	nolebatis	noluistis	noletis	nolueratis
they	nolunt	nolebant	noluerunt	nolent	noluerant
infinitive (*to*)	nolle				
imperatives:					
singular	noli				
plural	nolite				

SECTION 7: SYNTAX

Adverbs

Adverbs do not change their form in Latin. They will usually be found just before the verb at the end of the sentence.

servi <u>fortiter</u> pugnant.	pueri <u>semper</u> <u>bene</u> laborant.
The slaves fight <u>bravely</u>.	*Boys <u>always</u> work <u>well</u>.*

quod = *because* clauses

These are straightforward:

puella nautam amabat <u>quod</u> pecuniam habebat.	servi, <u>quod</u> dominum timebant, fugerunt.
The girl liked the sailor <u>because</u> he had money.	*<u>Because</u> the slaves were afraid of their master, they fled.*

ubi = *when* clauses

These also are straighforward:

servi, <u>ubi</u> pericula viderunt, cucurrerunt.
<u>When</u> the slaves saw the dangers, they ran.

The perfect indicative after **ubi** can be (and often is) translated as a pluperfect.

<u>ubi</u> magistrum vidit, perterritus erat.
<u>When</u> he saw/had seen the teacher, he was frightened.

Direct questions: –ne

A Latin statement can be changed into a question be adding **–ne** to the end of the first word of the sentence and adding a question mark to the end of the sentence:

1.	laborat.	*He is working.*
	laborat**ne**?	*Is he working?*
2.	est fessus.	*He is tired.*
	est**ne** fessus?	*Is he tired?*
3.	puer puellam spectat.	*The boy is looking at the girl.*
	puer**ne** puellam spectat?	*Is the boy looking at the girl?*

Present infinitives

You will find present infinitives used with the verbs **paro** = *prepare*, **cupio** = *want*, **constituo** = *decide* and **iubeo** = *order*. The infinitive usually comes just before the main verb at the end of the sentence.

puella <u>cantare</u> parat.	*The girl prepares to sing.*
pueri <u>ludere</u> cupiunt.	*The boys want to work.*
servi <u>pugnare</u> constituerunt.	*The slaves decided to fight.*
dominus servos <u>laborare</u> iussit.	*The master ordered the slaves to work.*

quamquam = *although* clauses

These are straightforward:

> quamquam femina pecuniam habebat, virum non habebat.
> *Although the woman had money, she did not have a husband.*
>
> milites, quamquam fessi erant, bene pugnaverunt.
> *Although the soldiers were tired, they fought well.*

Comparisons with quam = *than*

quam = *than* is used to compare things. The things being compared are always in the same case on either side of the **quam**.

> hic miles clarior quam ille erat.
> *This soldier was more famous than that one.*
>
> puellae sapientiores quam pueri sunt.
> *Girls are wiser than boys.*

Direct questions: nonne and num

nonne can be added to the start of a sentence to indicate that the answer 'yes' is expected. How you actually translate this word will depend on the sentence.

| nonne laborat? | *He is working, isn't he?* |
| | *Surely he is working?* |

num can be added to the start of a sentence to indicate that the answer 'no' is expected. How you actually translate this word will depend on the sentence.

num laborat?	*He is not working, is he?*
	Surely he is not working?

Prohibitions

Prohibitions are commands telling someone not to do something. In English they begin with the words 'Do not…'

In Latin singular prohibitions (telling one person not to do something) begin with the word **noli**.

Plural prohibitions (telling more than one person not to do something) begin with the word **nolite**.

The **noli/nolite** is followed by a present infinitive.

<u>noli</u> currere, puer!	<u>*Do not*</u> *run, boy!* (singular prohibition)
<u>nolite</u> currere, pueri!	<u>*Do not*</u> *run, boys!* (plural prohibition)

Reflexive pronouns

These are pronouns which reflect ('bend back') the action to the subject.

<u>me</u> cras necabo.	ille puer <u>se</u> amat.
I shall kill <u>myself</u> tomorrow.	*That boy likes <u>himself</u>.*
cur <u>vos</u> non defenditis, milites?	cives <u>se</u> hostibus tradiderunt.
Why are you not defending <u>yourselves</u>, soldiers?	*The citizens handed <u>themselves</u> over to the enemy.*

Time

There are three sorts of time expression in Latin.

1. Time how long   ACCUSATIVE endings.   mult<u>as</u> hor<u>as</u> dormivit.
   (key English word: *for*)   He slept <u>for</u> many hours.

2. Time when   ABLATIVE endings.   sext<u>a</u> hor<u>a</u> venit.
   (key English words: *in, at, on*)   He came <u>at</u> the sixth hour.

3. Time within which   ABLATIVE endings.   tri<u>bus</u> die<u>bus</u> advenit.
   (key English words: *within, in*)   He arrived <u>within</u> three days.

Place

	at	*towards*	*from*
normal nouns	prepositions + ablative in agro *in the field*	prepositions + accusative ad agrum *to the field*	prepositions + ablative ex agro *out of the field*
cities	locative* Romae *in/at Rome*	accusative only Romam *to Rome*	ablative only Roma *from Rome*

* For singular nouns of 1st and 2nd declensions, use genitive singular (eg Corinthi)
  For singular nouns of 3rd declension, use ablative singular (eg Carthagine)
  For plural nouns, use ablative plural (eg Athenis)

Relative clauses

The relative pronoun (**qui, quae, quod**) agrees with what it relates to in gender and number. Its case is determined by its function in the relative clause.

> puella, <u>quae</u> per viam ambulabat, pulchra erat.
> *The girl, <u>who</u> was walking along the road, was beautiful.*
>
> puella, <u>quam</u> specto, pulchra est.
> *The girl, <u>whom</u> I am looking at, is beautiful.*
>
> puella, <u>cuius</u> pater clarus est, pulchra est.
> *The girl, <u>whose</u> father is famous, is beautiful.*
>
> puella, <u>cui</u> donum dedi, pulchra erat.
> *The girl, <u>to whom</u> I gave a present, was beautiful.*

Purpose clauses

In English these are introduced by 'in order to', 'to', or 'so as to'.
In Latin they are introduced by **ut** = *in order to* or **ne** = *in order not to*.
In the past tense you will find these clauses end with a verb in the imperfect subjunctive.

> venimus ut laboraremus.
> *We came in order to work.*
>
> milites venerunt ut pugnarent.
> *The soldiers came in order to fight.*
>
> servus effugiebat ne laboraret.
> *The slave was escaping in order not to work.*

Indirect commands

These are concerned with ordering (**impero** + dative) or persuading (**persuadeo** + dative) someone to do something.

In Latin they are introduced by **ut** = *to* or **ne** = *not to*.

In the past tense you will find these clauses end with a verb in the imperfect subjunctive.

> dominus servo imperavit ut laboraret.
> *The master ordered the slave to work.*
> dux militibus persuasit ne dormirent.
> *The general persuaded the soldiers not to sleep.*

SECTION 8: NUMERALS

Cardinal numbers 1–10

unus	*one*
duo	*two*
tres	*three*
quattuor	*four*
quinque	*five*
sex	*six*
septem	*seven*
octo	*eight*
novem	*nine*
decem	*ten*

Ordinal numbers 1st–10th

primus	*first*
secundus	*second*
tertius	*third*
quartus	*fourth*
quintus	*fifth*
sextus	*sixth*
septimus	*seventh*
octavus	*eighth*
nonus	*ninth*
decimus	*tenth*

LEVEL
1

Cardinal numbers 11–20

Level 2

undecim	*eleven*
duodecim	*twelve*
tredecim	*thirteen*
quattuordecim	*fourteen*
quindecim	*fifteen*
sedecim	*sixteen*
septendecim	*seventeen*
duodeviginti	*eighteen*
undeviginti	*nineteen*
viginti	*twenty*

Cardinal numbers 30–1000

Level 3

triginta	*thirty*
quadraginta	*forty*
quinquaginta	*fifty*
sexaginta	*sixty*
septuaginta	*seventy*
octoginta	*eighty*
nonaginta	*ninety*
centum	*a hundred*
mille	*a thousand*